THE HEYDAY OF THE TROLLEYBUS

Ian Allan Publishing

HOWARD J. PILTZ

First published 1994
First reprinted 1996
Second reprint 1999

ISBN 0 7110 2271 2

© Ian Allan Publishing Ltd 1994

Published by Ian Allan Publishing

an imprint of Ian Allan Publishing Ltd, Terminal House,
Shepperton, Surrey TW17 8AS.
Printed by Ian Allan Printing Ltd, Riverdene Business
Park, Hersham, Surrey KT12 4RG.

Code: 9908/B

Front cover: Two of Portsmouth's prewar AEC
661Ts with Cravens bodywork are pictured,
with No 230 closest to the camera, at Cosham.
Julian Thompson

Back cover: Although labelled 'Brighton, Hove &
District Transport', No 38 was, in fact, a
Corporation-owned AEC 661T with Weymann
bodywork that dated originally from 1939.
Julian Thompson

Title page: A second example of the batch of
prewar AEC 661Ts, No 273 (originally No 73
until 1938), is seen in immaculate condition.
Although numerically the largest batch of
trolleybuses delivered to Portsmouth, none of
these AEC 661Ts survives. Two Portsmouth trolleybuses do, however, exist in preservation:
No 201, the original AEC 661T of 1934, and
No 313, one of the last batch of vehicles (BUT
9611Ts) delivered in 1950-51. *Julian Thompson*

Introduction

'Trolleybuses! What are trolleybuses, Dad?'

What a sobering comment from the
author's 17-year-old son, on learning of the
preparation of this book, and me, a shame-
less trolleybus fanatic during the 1960s
and 1970s. That pearl of wisdom reminded
me that in Great Britain today the
trolleybus has disappeared not only from
our roads, but also from our minds and
vocabulary.

'So! what *was* a trolleybus?'

'Well, son, in the days before North Sea
oil, when all of our oil was imported,
trolleybuses ran on electricity made from
home-produced coal. They were silent, so
much so that some thought them
positively dangerous, and they were pollution free in operation.'

Trolleybuses saw their genesis in the
need for public transport when demand
was insufficient to justify either a tramway
or a railway in an age before the
establishment of the internal combustion
engine as a wholly viable alternative. The
first tentative steps in the UK, with
primitive equipment, saw vehicles
experimentally operated in both Hove and
London, whilst representatives of several
operators travelled abroad to see the
trolleybus in operation in several
European countries. In June 1911 the
neighbouring West Riding cities of Leeds
and Bradford organised a co-ordinated
inauguration of 'trackless trams' or
'tracklesses' as tramway feeders. The
technology leant heavily on tramway prac-
tices and the vehicles also owed much to
their larger cousins to such an extent that
the drivers of these early vehicles were
required to wrestle with a hand-operated
controller (similar to those installed in
contemporary tramcars) whilst struggling
with quite unsophisticated steering that
kicked and fought according to the whim
of the unmetalled roads, problems that
were compounded by the solid tyres of the
early trolleybuses. Dust was a severe
problem and was a major factor in the
demise of the Dundee operation, where the
one route, two vehicle system lasted only
two years from 1912 to 1914, thus making
this Scottish city the first place to abandon
this new form of transport.

In spite of the early problems the trolleybus survived. Whilst some of the early systems fell by the wayside — Leeds decided
to concentrate on developing its tramway
system and thus abandoned the trolleybus
routes finally in 1928 — others prospered,
most notably in Bradford where the
municipal burghers persevered and
bequeathed to the city a transport system
second-to-none. Other early operators,
such as Rotherham and Teesside, were
also to be amongst the longest lasting
systems in the country.

Through the immediate post World
War 1 period the trolleybus continued to
develop. The first covered-top double-deck
vehicle appeared in 1920 and the first tram
to trolleybus conversion followed shortly
thereafter. The passenger carrying capacity
of the trolleybus was now starting to rival
that of the tram and it was little wonder
that systems such as Wolverhampton and
Nottingham inaugurated conversion
programmes during the 1920s.

Compared to the contemporary

motorbus, a trolleybus had the advantage of almost limitless supplies of power from an external source and, in an age when municipal enterprise was appreciated, this power could be drawn from municipally-owned power stations. The trolleybus's power made it particularly suited to hilly routes such as are found in Huddersfield and Bradford, or with its excellent acceleration to services where frequent stops were necessary.

Due to the lack of engine vibration, high temperatures and pressures, the trolleybus tended to last longer than the equivalent motorbus, and often had its life extended still further by rebodying. One of the two trolleybuses specially repainted by Bradford City Transport in 1961, No 603, achieved more than 1,000,000 miles in service from construction in 1934 until its withdrawal in 1962. Maintenance was also less demanding and, as a result, trolleybuses were able to withstand wartime abuses during World War 2 much more effectively than a contemporary motorbus.

Respectability for the trolleybus in Britain finally came when, after the initial London United conversions of 1931, the newly-created London Passenger Transport Board adopted the vehicle for its tramway conversion programme. The LPTB appreciated not only the superior development of the trolleybus for use in the hurly-burly of the capital's traffic, but also its ability to utilise the existing infrastructure of power generation and distribution that had been constructed for the trams. Conversions continued through until the early years of the war, by which time London could lay claim to the largest single trolleybus network in the world. If war had not intervened the remaining tram routes would also have been converted but, by the time of 'Operation Tramaway' in 1950-52, the trolleybus was no longer in favour.

So what happened to turn the tide against the trolleybus? The unpalatable fact has got to be acknowledged that just as London gave credibility to the trolleybus prior to World War 2, so the capital's decision to replace them likewise dealt a fatal blow to the long-term outlook for this mode of transport. In London, the postwar conversions were from tram to motorbus rather than to trolleybus. Trolleybuses were no longer as cheap to buy or operate as motorbuses and, with such types as London's own RT or the Leyland Titan, there were now bus chassis more readily able to provide the level of reliability required. Pollution was not then perceived as the issue it is today, the electricity supply industry had been recently Nationalised — meaning that there was now less incentive to maintain electrically-operated vehicles — and the overhead, so essential to the trolleybus, was becoming a liability. The costs of extending routes to the new suburban housing estates meant that these were increasingly served by bus, whilst in London the trolleybus had never really penetrated the central area, lacking the tram's ability to utilise the conduit supply in areas where the erection of overhead was undesirable.

So, the trolleybus was no longer fashionable and in many towns and cities this made it very easy to allow the arguments in council chambers and board rooms to swing so easily against the trolleybus. There is no doubt that many factors mounted up to help sway the argument: vehicle costs were rising as volume production of chassis wound down; the costs of overhead maintenance and renewal were also increasing as was the price of electricity; the motorbus was now a proven product; towns and cities were eager to undertake the wholesale redevelopment of centres and trolleybuses were not perceived as desirable during the construction of major new roads. Despite the warning given by the Suez crisis of 1956, where restrictions on the use of oil emphasised the problems of relying on an imported source of fuel, the late 1950s and 1960s were to witness an inexorable decline in Britain's trolleybus operations.

One by one trolleybus systems closed in favour of the diesel bus. Whilst some fell easily, even the committed operators — Bournemouth, Reading, Teesside and Walsall — finally bowed to the inevitable as spares dried-up and new vehicles became unavailable. Gradually the major strongholds fell — Nottingham in 1966, Reading in 1968, Bournemouth (despite the acquisition of new vehicles in 1962) in 1969 and both Cardiff and Walsall in 1970. Although opening an extension as late as 1968 and acquiring a number of vehicles second-hand from Reading in 1969, Britain's penultimate system, Teesside, was converted to bus operation in April 1971.

The final tragedy of them all occurred in March 1972 when the last operator — Bradford — bade farewell to a form of transport that had faithfully served the city for more than 60 years. As the town-hall carillon played 'Auld Lang Syne' the last trolleybus to run on a British street, No 844, made its stately way back to Thornbury depot on the afternoon of the 26th — a day indelibly ingrained on the memory of all those who witnessed the demise of the British trolleybus. *Requiescat in pace.*

3

Ashton-under-Lyne

Left: The Ashton-under-Lyne municipality was one of Britain's pioneering trolleybus operators. In 1925 it linked up with Oldham for a jointly operated service on the hilly route between the two towns via Hathershawe, using solid-tyred 'Railless' single-deck vehicles that played havoc with the road surface to such an extent that the following year saw Oldham revert to tramcars for their portion of the service. Undeterred, Ashton continued with its truncated route long enough to see various trial runs by new double-deckers (including some of Manchester's) being readied for further conversions to trolleybuses of routes to Manchester in 1937. No 80 seen here was one of five Crossley Empires with Crossley bodywork purchased by Ashton in 1950. This particular vehicle survived long enough to be purchased for preservation and, at the time of writing, was approaching the end of an extensive rebuild at the Museum of Transport, Manchester. *Author*

Right: Ashton No 87 was one of the final batch of vehicles purchased, being part of a series of eight (Nos 82-89) of 1956. The chassis supplier was BUT (of the 9612T type) and bodywork was supplied by the local firm of S. H. Bond. The scene here is Aytoun Street not long before the final closure of the system in 1966. Alongside is Manchester bus No 4630, one of that operator's last conventional Daimler CVG6s delivered in 1963, whilst on the extreme right it is possible, in the 1990s, to witness Manchester's newest form of public transport, the Metrolink. *Author*

Belfast

Left: There was no more majestic backdrop for a British trolleybus than Stormont Castle in Belfast, where overhead wires completely encircled the Northern Ireland parliament building. The only trolleybus system on the island, Belfast's was also a relatively late operator of this form of transport, with the system being inaugurated in 1938 with a fleet of 14 varied types purchased for assessment. The bulk of the city's postwar fleet was made up of Guy BTXs and BUT 9641T six-wheelers. No 144 seen here was a Guy which had entered service in 1948. *F. W. Ivey*

Right: These immensely handsome trolleybuses represent examples of Guy and BUT trolleybuses that were bodied by the Ulster firm of Harkness. No 99 was a prewar AEC 664T whilst No 203 represented a postwar BUT 9641T. *F. W. Ivey*

Below right: Harkness bodied the vast majority of buses and trolleybuses used in Belfast well into the 1970s and the family resemblance is clearly visible here as a prewar AEC and a postwar BUT stand alongside No 534, an ex-London Transport Daimler rebodied by Harkness and GZ4011. *F. W. Ivey*

Bournemouth

Above: Like Belfast, Bournemouth experimented in the early days with a small number of different trolleybuses. One type tested, the Sunbeam MS2, was perpetuated through the acquisition of no fewer than 102 almost identical vehicles with luxuriously-appointed dual-door bodies. Here No 97 (later renumbered 211) is seen turning on to the well-known turntable at Christchurch. More than 20 years after the end of trolleybus operation in the borough, the turntable still survives behind a modern shopping development. *Author's Collection*

Right: No 274 was a Weymann-bodied Sunbeam MF2B, one of a batch of 39 vehicles delivered in three stages between 1958 and 1962. These modern-looking vehicles were the last new trolleybuses to be delivered to a British operator. Unfortunately, their life was to be short and by the time of their withdrawal the market for second-hand vehicles had all but dried up. As a result the majority of these fine trolleybuses passed to the scrapman; a number, however, survive in preservation. *Author*

Left: The wake for the closure of the Bournemouth system turned out to be more of a celebration than a requiem, and in April 1969 hordes of enthusiasts came with preserved buses or trolleybuses for final tours. Seen at the Corporation's Mallard Road depot are Nos 202 (one of the three early Sunbeams converted to open-top form in 1958), 246 (a Weymann-bodied BUT 9641T dating back to 1950) and 301 (a Sunbeam MF2B of 1962). The last of the trio had the distinction of being one of the last three trolleybuses built for service in Britain. It was destined to join the other two vehicles seen here in preservation. *Author*

Below left: Being a relatively late survivor, Bournemouth was able to take advantage of the availability of serviceable vehicles that had been replaced by diesel buses elsewhere, and it is somewhat fitting that the only vehicles acquired came from that other seaside resort just down the road — Brighton. The latter town provided seven identical Weymann-bodied BUT 9611Ts, four from the Corporation fleet and three from the fleet of Brighton, Hove & District. The vehicles became Nos 288-91 (ex-Brighton Corporation) and Nos 292-4 (ex-BHD). All seven entered service in Bournemouth in 1959 and were withdrawn six years later. *John Senior*

Right: The Square is the focus of all local roads in the town and, in consequence, plays an important part in the provision of public transport. In the 1990s this scene has changed greatly, but here we see a view of how we all like to remember the town — sun, flowers and spotless, fume-free trolleybuses. BUT No 244, one of a batch of 9641Ts delivered in 1950 and originally numbered 210, is caught passing the bottom of Richmond Hill. This exceptionally steep road was eminently suitable for trolleybuses; and ironically in the 1990s it has been pedestrianised. On the right a prewar Leyland, with full-front Weymann bodywork, was typical of the resort's bus fleet. *John Senior*

Bradford

Left: To wool city of Bradford goes the distinction, along with the neighbouring city of Leeds, of inaugurating the first trolleybus system in the country on 20 June 1911. Sixty-one years later, on 26 March 1972, Bradford was also to witness the demise of trolleybus operation.

No 738 was a Karrier W supplied in 1946 and fitted with a Roe-built Utility body. Like so many Bradford vehicles, No 738 was to undergo rebodying, it received a front-entrance body supplied by East Lancs in 1959 and survived in service until 1970. The vehicle is seen with its original bodywork awaiting departure with a service to Clayton. The impressive bulk of Bradford's Town Hall dominates the background. *John Senior*

Right: In 1961 Bradford celebrated the 50th anniversary of its trolleybus system. To mark this milestone, two trolleybuses were repainted into historic liveries. No 687, a 1938 Karrier with English Electric bodywork, was restored to its original livery, whilst No 603, a 1934 AEC 661T (originally fitted with an English Electric body, but rebodied by Northern Coachbuilders after World War 2), was completed in a version of the 1911 livery. The latter is seen awaiting departure on a service to Clayton. Although both would have made ideal preservation candidates, neither was to survive. *Photobus/A. Richardson*

Left: During the 1950s, under the inspired management of C. T. Humpidge, the Bradford system underwent considerable expansion and modernisation. From the mid-1950s significant numbers of vehicles — such as No 651, an AEC 661T of 1938 — were rebodied by East Lancs. To the right of No 651 is Karrier W No 737, which is seen with its original Utility body. No 737, along with the rest of the 'DKY' batch of Karriers, was also to receive a new East Lancs body. The scene is Thornbury depot and the date is 4 August 1958. Although No 651 has long since succumbed, No 737 is, fortunately, still around and is displayed in Bradford's Industrial Museum, where it can be seen alongside Bradford's only surviving tram. *John Senior*

Right: Bradford's determination to exploit the virtues of trolleybuses meant that the Corporation was in the happy position of being able to take advantage of other systems as they closed. Thus Bradford became the home to many trolleybuses, unwanted by their original operators but still with many years of useful life left.

One of the operators that was to supply second-hand vehicles was the company-owned Notts & Derby system which closed in 1953. A total of some 32 headed north; of these 10 received new East Lancs rear-entrance bodies, whilst the remainder retained their original bodywork. Amongst the latter was No 773 a BUT 9611T dating from 1949 and originally No 356 in the Notts & Derby fleet. It was to remain in service until October 1963. Two sister vehicles, Nos 770 and 774, have been preserved. *John Senior*

Above: Another supplier of second-hand vehicles was St Helens. No 798 was a BUT 9611T supplied new in 1951 with an East Lancs rear-entrance body. Eight vehicles were sold to Bradford, becoming Nos 794-801. No 798 is seen here on Hall Ings in the company of an East Lancs-bodied AEC. The hoardings hide the redevelopment of the old Lancashire & Yorkshire Railway Bridge Street goods depot. Part of the site was later occupied by the Norfolk Gardens Hotel and part by the Transport Interchange. *Author*

Right: Other places to supply second-hand trolleybuses to Bradford included Hastings, Brighton, Darlington, Doncaster and Llanelli. Vehicles were also acquired from Ashton and Grimsby-Cleethorpes, but these never entered service. The last acquisitions — indeed the last vehicles to enter service in the city — were seven Sunbeam S4 single-deckers from Mexborough & Swinton. A further five were also acquired but were never used.

The batch, Nos 841-7, were rebodied by East Lancs before entering service in 1962-63. Here, No 844, bearing the dual legend 'Bradford's Last Trolleybus' on the front and 'Britain's Last Trolleybus' on the side, performs the last rites on 26 March 1972. The author's abiding memory of that Sunday afternoon was of the hairs on the back of his neck standing up as the carillon of Bradford Town Hall played 'Auld Lang Syne' as No 844 departed for Thornbury depot for the last time. Inevitably, No 844, along with three others of the batch, survives in preservation. *Author*

Brighton

Left: Although the seaside town of Brighton was to witness one of the earliest experiments in trolleybus operation, it was not destined to see a system inaugurated until May 1939. The background to the construction of this relatively late operation was the creation of a joint working area in the town between the Corporation and the Brighton, Hove & District company fleet. As part of the arrangement, Brighton's tramway system was to be converted to trolleybus operation and BH&D was to have the right to operate a maximum of 20% of the annual mileage. A total of 52 trolleybuses was acquired by the Corporation between 1939 and 1953, whilst BH&D supplied eight (which entered service in 1946). A final extension was constructed in 1951, but in 1956 the decision was taken to convert the system to bus operation. The routes were converted between 1959 and 30 June 1961.

The main town centre terminus was at Old Steine and No 20, one of the original Corporation batch of AEC 661Ts with Weymann bodies supplied in 1939, is seen at this central location with a service for Preston Drove. *Geoff Lumb*

Right: Another of the original batch, No 40, is caught heading towards Old Steine over the postwar Hollingbury route. Following withdrawal, four of Brighton's vehicles were sold to Bournemouth, two to Bradford and two to Maidstone. One of the last mentioned, No 52, was subsequently preserved as was one of the BH&D AECs. *Julian Thompson*

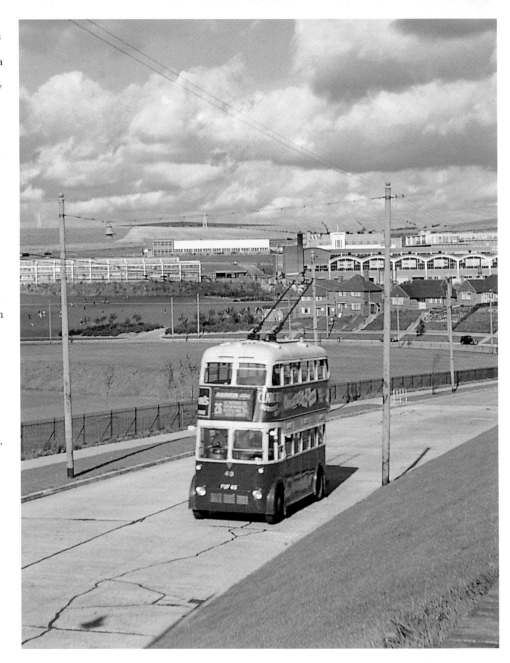

Cardiff

Left: The capital city of Wales was another city that adopted trolleybuses late in the day, in this case March 1942 following a decision taken just prior to the outbreak of war to replace the tram network. The tramway system had been afflicted from the earliest days with the problem of low railway bridges, and the trolleybuses were to face the same difficulty. As a result Cardiff operated a number of single-deck vehicles — never particularly common latterly amongst British operators — on a route along Bute Street. Originally ex-Pontypridd vehicles were used, but these were replaced by BUT 9641Ts fitted with East Lancs single-deck bodies in 1949-50, such as No 241 illustrated here. *F. W. Ivey*

Above: In 1949 Cardiff introduced a batch of 20 BUT 9641Ts, Nos 245-64 as the system expanded following the withdrawal of the remaining trams. These vehicles were either fitted with East Lancs bodywork or with bodywork constructed by Bruce Coachworks on East Lancs body frames. Two of the latter, Nos 247 and 262, are seen. No 262 was subsequently to be preserved on withdrawal in 1965. *Michael Allen*

Derby

Left: The railway town of Derby, famous as the home of the Midland Railway, inaugurated its first trolleybus route on 9 January 1932. The system expanded rapidly during the 1930s and extensions continued to be built through both the World War 2 period and the immediate postwar years. The first withdrawal, however, occurred in 1950, although the wiring remained until 1962. Further extensions brought the system to its maximum extent in 1958. Conversion started in 1960 and the final trolleybuses operated in February 1967.

The fleet consisted mainly of three-axle vehicles prewar, but two-axle types predominated after 1944. The last new vehicles were eight Sunbeam F4As acquired in 1959-60, which were fitted with Roe bodies. Despite these modern vehicles, Derby was also to play host to the final Utility trolleybuses operated in public service. Here we see No 172, which was later to be preserved, a Park Royal-bodied Sunbeam W delivered originally in 1945. *F. W. Ivey*

Above: Derby was also notable in the system's latter days for its remarkably slack overhead wiring; trolleybuses would noticeably push the overhead up as they passed underneath. In addition, much redundant wiring was left intact after early route closures, which allowed for the coverage of long-disused wiring on the final day's operation. Shortly before the final withdrawal, examples of two types of postwar Derby trolleybus are pictured: No 203 is a 1948 Sunbeam F4 with Brush bodywork, whilst No 229 was a 1953 Sunbeam F4 with Willowbrook body. Examples of both types survive in preservation. *F. W. Ivey*

23

Doncaster

Left: Like Derby, the South Yorkshire town of Doncaster was and is proud of its railway heritage, with its locomotive workshops producing such famous engines as *Flying Scotsman* and *Mallard*. The town could also claim a significant trolleybus network that was to last more than three decades. A total of 68 trolleybuses were acquired from 1928, when the system was inaugurated, and the outbreak of war in 1939. These vehicles included a rare Bristol trolleybus — No 31 which lasted from 1931 until 1945 — as well as the products of more common chassis manufacturers such as Karrier. Postwar the fleet was modernised with vehicles supplied from mainly Karrier and Sunbeam, although a number of second-hand BUTs were acquired from Darlington (these were later sold to Bradford). Other second-hand vehicles were acquired and rebodied by Roe, who also rebodied many of the system's postwar vehicles. No 375, which is now preserved at Sandtoft, was a Karrier W supplied to Doncaster in 1945 with a Park Royal body. It was rebodied in the mid-1950s. *F. W. Ivey*

Right: From the earliest trolleybuses delivered, the Leeds firm of Charles H. Roe supplied the majority of bodies. Apart from the East Lancs-bodied BUTs received from Darlington, the remaining second-hand acquisitions were all rebodied by Roe between 1956 and 1959. The last two trolleybuses to enter service, in 1958, were two ex-Mexborough & Swinton single-deckers that received Roe double-deck bodies. Here one of the duo, No 353, is seen in the company of Daimler CVG6 No 163. These later Roe trolleybus bodies were noteworthy in that as they were withdrawn 20 of the bodies were transferred to new motor bus chassis. The tell-tale feature that identified these bodies later in their life was the strengthened, wider window pillar visible on No 353 behind the first upper-deck window on each side. One of the buses that received an ex-trolleybus body has subsequently been preserved. *F. W. Ivey*

Glasgow

Above: To Glasgow, the largest city in Scotland and the home of many of the greatest engineering works in the country, goes the distinction of being the last trolleybus system to open in Britain as well as being the last city in the country where trolleybuses could operate alongside trams. Trolleybuses, however, never appeared at home amongst the severe and overpowering tenement blocks so characteristic of this proud city, whilst the trams had always seemed almost implanted in the city streets. Trolleybuses arrived in Glasgow in 1949 and the first vehicles to be delivered were a batch of 34 BUT 9641Ts and 30 Daimler CTMEs bodied by MCCW to London's 'Q1' design to speed delivery after the war. One of the Daimlers, No TD16, is seen against the characteristic tenement blocks, buildings blackened through the grime of the industrial age. *F. W. Ivey*

Right: The well-known Scottish body building firm of Alexanders was to build the bodywork for many of Glasgow's buses but only ever supplied five trolleybus bodies which, inevitably, were fitted to vehicles constructed for Glasgow. The bodies were fitted to Nos TG1-5, Sunbeam F4As delivered in 1953. Sunbeams Nos TG6-10 received bodywork by Weymann and Nos TG5 and TG12 are seen together. *F. W. Ivey*

Left: The final double-deck deliveries to Glasgow, in 1957-59, were 60 BUT 9613Ts, Nos TB65-124, which were constructed to the recently authorised increased length of 30ft for two-axle vehicles. These trolleybuses, fitted with bodywork by Crossley, were amongst the last vehicles to receive bodies from that Stockport manufacturer. No TB78, which is now preserved at the Sandtoft Transport Centre, is caught painted in a shortlived version of the ever-evolving Glasgow livery, whilst two other members of the same type exhibit what was nearer to the then standard livery. Following the abandonment of the tramway network in 1962, the trolleybus network was converted to bus operation over a number of years with the last routes being replaced in March 1967. *F. W. Ivey*

Above right: Glasgow's first single-deck trolleybus was delivered in 1951. It was followed in 1953 by a batch of 10 BUT RETB1s with East Lancs bodywork. Initially these were constructed as dual-door vehicles with only 27 seats, but this proved unpopular and by the time No TBS7 was photographed on 18 May 1964 all had been converted to single-door with 36 seats. *Geoff Lumb*

Below right: Amongst the notable developments undertaken by Glasgow Corporation was the introduction of a batch of 10 35ft-long single-deck trolleybuses, Nos TBS12-21, in 1958. These Burlingham-bodied BUT RETB1s only entered service with special dispensation from the Ministry of Transport as they exceeded the existing maximum permitted length for two-axle vehicles. Designed for use on route No 108, the batch was withdrawn between 1961 and 1967. No TBS13, seen here in the Museum at Coplawhill, was preserved by the Corporation. A second example, No TBS21, also survives. *John Senior*

Grimsby-Cleethorpes

Left: The neighbouring east coast systems of Grimsby and Cleethorpes merged into a single entity in early 1957, formalising an arrangement for interworking that had existed for many years. Grimsby was the first of the two to introduce trolleybuses — in 1926 — whilst Cleethorpes followed suit a decade later in 1937 after the latter had taken over the remains of the Great Grimsby Street Tramways Co. The system was relatively small — Cleethorpes only possessed a total of 15 vehicles over 20 years and Grimsby 26 over 30 — and the first conversion to bus operation had taken place prior to the creation of the joint undertaking. Formal closure of the remains of the system was proposed in October 1959 and the system was converted to bus operation in January 1960.

Seen in the joint operation's livery is No 64, one of two Roe-bodied Crossley 'Empires' delivered new to Cleethorpes in 1951 and sold to Walsall in 1960. Whilst its sister, No 63, survived almost long enough to witness the demise of the Walsall system, No 64 was subjected to a trial to see if a diesel engine could be persuaded to work from the rear platform. As No 873 it languished for quite some time with much of the rear lower-deck cut away before, thankfully, being consigned for scrap. *Photobus/A. Richardson*

Right: An almost forgotten — but still essential — part of any trolleybus operation was the tower wagon; these vehicles were of vital importance in the erection, maintenance and eventually the destruction of each and every trolleybus operation. Initially, vehicles were inherited from those that had serviced the tram fleet — often horse-powered — but in later years a rich variety of purpose-built or converted wagons appeared. Typical is this example in the fleet of Grimsby-Cleethorpes seen, just before the system's closure, in April 1960. EE 8128 started life as a Roe-bodied Albion single-deck bus in 1927. *Geoff Lumb*

Hastings

Left: Public transport in the south coast seaside resort of Hastings was provided by the Hastings Tramways Co. Despite opposition from the local council, which had not exercised its option to acquire the system in the mid-1920s, the company obtained powers in 1927 to replace the trams with trolleybuses. The first route was inaugurated in 1928 and the system quickly expanded. The company became a subsidiary of Maidstone & District in 1935 and a new green livery was adopted at that time, although the vehicles retained 'Hastings Tramway Company' lettering until it was formally merged with M&D in 1957. It was also in 1957 that the policy of conversion to bus operation was announced and the entire system was abandoned over a two year period. The last vehicle ran on 1 June 1959.

A total of 58 Guys were acquired between 1928 and 1930 to operate the system. These were replaced by a number of new trolleybuses acquired between 1940 and 1948. However, one of the original batch of open-top double-deck Guy BTXs with Dodson bodywork, No 3, was to survive to be restored in 1953 (as No 3A) and continued in public service until the demise of the system. It survived in operation after 1959 through the fitting of a diesel engine. It is pictured in its restored state, in the brown livery that the Hastings company used before the 1935 take-over. *Julian Thompson*

Right: One of the 1946 batch of Sunbeam Ws with Park Royal bodywork, No 21, is seen on circular route No 2. Notice the complete lack of other traffic with the exception of the cyclist on the left. No 21, along with another 11 Hastings trolleybuses, was sold to Bradford Corporation in 1959. It became No 806 in the Yorkshire fleet. Like the rest of the ex-Hastings vehicles, it was, however, to have only a relatively short life in Yorkshire, being withdrawn for scrap in November 1962. *Julian Thompson*

Left: A side view of No 31, a Sunbeam W with Weymann body delivered in 1948, showing clearly the ownership of Maidstone & District. The batch of 15 vehicles bought in 1948, Nos 31-45, represented the last trolleybuses acquired by the company. No 31, along with seven others, was sold to Walsall in 1959; five others were sold to Maidstone. *Julian Thompson*

Huddersfield

Above: Another operator to appreciate the hill-climbing abilities of the trolleybus was Huddersfield. It was the closure of this system in 1968 that drew the author's attention to the

fact that the continual erosion of the number of trolleybus operators in this country would inevitably lead to the eventual extinction of the breed. Magnificent red and cream vehicles that served the town impeccably for almost 45 years and had been maintained in outstanding condition were sacrificed to the all-pervading diesel bus. An interesting feature of the Huddersfield system was the turntable built out on to the Pennine hillside way above the town at Longwood. Looking terribly dangerous, the high winds caught one trolleybus and, according to local folklore, spun it round many times. Legend does not recall how it was stopped or

the comments of the crew. Later, another trolleybus was reversed off the turntable and appeared in the local press on its side in a most undignified position. The turntable had already been locked by this date and was used as a reversing point only.

Typical of the Huddersfield fleet is this Park Royal-bodied Karrier MS2 dating from 1949. The three-window design on the front of the top-deck was characteristic of early Huddersfield trolleybuses, including No 541 (now preserved), although later vehicles (as well as those earlier vehicles rebodied) had a more conventional double-window. *F. W. Ivey*

Left: No 578, one of a batch of Karrier MS2s delivered in 1949, is seen climbing The Ainleys on its way from West Vale and Elland into town on St George's Day 1960. Originally fitted with a Park Royal body, No 578 was one of 69 vehicles rebodied by either Roe or East Lancs between 1950 and 1963; in this case No 578 has a Roe body. *Geoff Lumb*

Above: The penultimate batch of trolleybuses to be delivered to Huddersfield were 12 BUT 9641Ts with East Lancs bodywork delivered in 1956. One of the batch is pictured in the spring of 1965. Sister vehicle No 619 is preserved. *Geoff Lumb*

Ipswich

Above: The council of the Suffolk town of Ipswich was keen to maintain the use of electric transport even though the tramway system was becoming inefficient with much trackwork requiring renewal. There was also, in the era before bus regulation, the threat of local bus operators eager to receive local support. All these factors made the introduction of trolleybuses inevitable. The first trial runs were made in September 1923 and the system quickly expanded. Following the abandonment of the last trams, Ipswich could claim an all-trolleybus operation — a situation which persisted through until 1950. A total of 85 trolleybuses were acquired by 1939, of which all bar four were supplied by the local firms of Ransomes, Sims & Jefferies and Garretts. After World War 2 the fleet was renewed through the acquisition of new Sunbeam and Karrier types. However, following the introduction of the first diesel bus in 1950 and the first

conversion from trolleybus to motorbus in 1953, the whole system was converted by August 1963.

No 103 was one of a batch of six Karrier Ws introduced in 1948-49 and fitted with Park Royal bodywork. This company supplied the bodywork for all Ipswich's postwar acquisitions. *F. W. Ivey*

Right: In 1950 a final batch of new trolleybuses was acquired — 12 Sunbeam F4s, Nos 115-126. One of this final batch, No 119, is seen on Fore Street on the last day of the system's operation, 23 August 1963. Eight of the batch, including No 121, were sold for further service in Walsall and the last, No 126, was subsequently preserved. Note the unique brushed aluminium sides that were a feature of the Ipswich livery. *Michael Allen*

Kingston-upon-Hull

Left: The east coast port city of Kingston-upon-Hull took powers to replace its tramway system with trolleybuses in 1936, although there had been an earlier (and aborted) scheme almost a decade earlier. The first route to be inaugurated was, however, the motorbus route to Chanterlands Avenue, which commenced operation on 23 July 1937. By the outbreak of war a fleet of 66 vehicles was in operation, with chassis supplied by Karrier, Sunbeam and Crossley. The system continued to grow, reaching a maximum fleet size of 100 in 1948. Although new vehicles were acquired as late as 1955, conversion began in 1961 and the final route succumbed to the diesel bus in October 1964.

No 96, seen crossing the North Bridge on the Holderness Road route, was one of a batch of 10 Sunbeam F4s with Roe bodies acquired in 1948. The Holderness Road route was the only service that headed east from the town over the North Bridge; it was converted to bus operation in September 1963. *F. W. Ivey*

Below left: The last trolleybuses delivered to Hull were 16 Sunbeam MF2Bs with Roe bodies supplied between 1953 and 1955. The first was No 101, which was delivered in 1953 — Coronation year — and the type thus became known as 'Coronations'. The set-back front axle, seen here on No 103, allowed for the front door by the driver. Unfortunately, the conversion programme of 1961-64 meant that these fine vehicles had a tragically short life. Although they were offered for sale at closure, there were no takers and the entire batch was scrapped. *F. W. Ivey*

Right: Another 'Coronation', No 102, is pictured on the Beverley Road route at one of the numerous level crossings that were such a feature of the Hull system. Trolleybuses were to have a 26-year life on this route, replacing trams in September 1938 before being themselves replaced by motor buses on 31 October 1964 — the last route to be converted. *F. W. Ivey*

London

Left: At its peak the trolleybus network in London operated some 1,800 vehicles making it, by far, the largest system in Britain and, for a period, in the world. Although there had been experiments as early as 1909 in the metropolis, it was not until London United Tramways inaugurated its network of routes in the Kingston area in 1931 that public services commenced. Following the creation of the London Passenger Transport Board in 1933, the trolleybus became the chosen form of vehicle for tramcar replacement and the majority of routes in north and east London were converted between then and 1940. The war intervened to prevent the conversion of the southern routes and these were later converted to bus operation. Whilst there was a minor conversion in the early 1950s as a result of the abandonment of the tramway network, the decision to convert the trolleybus network to bus operation came in 1954. Formal conversion started in March 1959 and the last routes were converted in May 1962.

The LPTB inherited 61 trolleybuses from LUT in 1933 and in 1934 acquired two further experimental vehicles. The first major orders for vehi-cles from the LPTB went to Leyland, who supplied 30 'B1s' in 1935-36 (Nos 64-93), and to AEC. One of the Leyland vehicles, No 82, was photographed whilst operating on route No 654 to Sutton. *Julian Thompson*

Above: No 1366 seen here on route No 513 to Holborn Circus was one of a batch of 15 Class L1s introduced in 1939. Sister vehicle No 1365 was one of several casualties resulting from wartime damage. Route No 513 succumbed to the all-conquering motorbus in January 1961. *Julian Thompson*

43

Left: During World War 2 London, along with Bradford, was to receive a number of trolleybuses which had been diverted from orders for operators in South Africa. A total of 43 vehicles were received by London of which 25 Leylands had been ordered by Durban and 18 AECs by Johannesburg. Built to South African specifications, these vehicles were 8ft wide rather than the then maximum permitted width in the UK of 7ft 6in. No 1763, captured on route No 693 to Barking Broadway, was one of the AEC 664Ts for Johannesburg which were classified SA3 in London. Fitted with Metro-Cammell bodywork, the type entered service in 1942-43. *Julian Thompson*

Right: The last new trolleybuses delivered to London Transport, in 1948 to 1952, were the 'Q1' class of BUT 9641Ts fitted with Metro-Cammell bodywork, Nos 1765-1891. Designed to replace the original vehicles supplied in the early 1930s, the 'Q1s' were to be the only trolleybuses delivered to London after 1945. No 1769 is pictured heading towards Hampton Court on route No 604 past Wimbledon Town Hall. *Julian Thompson*

Below right: A second 'Q1', No 1808, heads towards Hampton Court on route No 667. Although the original closure plan of 1954 envisaged the survival of the ex-LUT routes until the expiry of the 'Q1' type's life, when it proved possible to export the vehicles to operators in Spain, the whole system was condemned. All the 'Q1s' with a couple of exceptions — one for preservation — were exported in 1960-61. Subsequently, a second example has been repatriated for preservation. *Julian Thompson*

Maidstone

Above: The town of Maidstone, set astride the River Medway, is the county town of Kent. Powers to operate trolleybuses were acquired in the early 1920s and the first route, in replacement of the existing trams, to Barming commenced operation with vehicles supplied by Ransomes, Sims & Jefferies in 1928. Although the Maidstone system was always small, it can lay claim to one of the last extensions to be built in Britain — around the Parkwood estate in 1963. However, in 1964 a four-year conversion scheme was announced and the system was to close in April 1967.

As elsewhere, Maidstone took advantage of the decline in other systems to acquire second-hand vehicles. One of a pair of ex-Brighton Weymann-bodied BUT 9611Ts, No 51 (ironically also No 51 in the Brighton fleet) is seen at the Fountain Inn, a short working of the route to Barming. Sister vehicle No 52 is preserved as the only Brighton Corporation trolleybus to survive. Other second-hand vehicles came from Hastings and Llanelli. *F. W. Ivey*

Right: The last batch of completely new trolleybuses acquired by Maidstone was a series of 12 Sunbeam Ws with Northern Coach Builders bodywork supplied in 1946 and 1947. One of the batch, No 64, heads for the immortally-named terminus at Loose. *Geoff Lumb*

Above: No 67 is a second example of the final batch of all-new trolleybuses acquired after World War 2. A number of Maidstone trolleybuses survive in preservation, including No 72, the last of this batch of vehicles. *F. W. Ivey*

Manchester

Below: The Manchester trolleybus system, which commenced operation in 1938, was the end result of a period of controversy between the city council, which wished to see the introduction of trolleybuses, and the Transport Committee, advised by the then General Manager (R. Stuart Pilcher), who wished to see the remaining trams converted to motorbus operation. In the event, Manchester's commitment to trolleybus operation was never more than half-hearted and only a relatively small network — closely linked with that of neighbouring Ashton — developed. Although a final batch of new trolleybuses was acquired in 1955, the first closures also occurred in that year. The conversion of the system was completed in December 1966.

Not surprisingly, the local manufacturer — Crossley — was given several orders for vehicles, the firm supplying 134 chassis between 1938 and 1951. These vehicles also had Crossley bodies. No 1242, seen here on route No 210 to Hyde and Gee Cross, was one of a batch of 16 TDD64/1 'Dominions' supplied in 1951. Sister vehicle No 1250 is one of two Manchester trolleybuses to survive into preservation. *Author's Collection*

Left: Seen at Audenshaw are vehicles belonging to both Manchester and Ashton-under-Lyne. Routes Nos 215 and 216 used Ashton New Road whilst Nos 218 and 219 used Ashton Old Road. Although Ashton was empowered to operate along both of these roads, it chose to operate only on the latter. Ashton No 84 was a BUT 9612T delivered in 1955 with Bond bodywork, whilst Manchester No 1325 was also a BUT 9612T, delivered in the mid-1950s, but fitted with a Burlingham body. *Author*

Above: The last batch of trolleybuses delivered to Manchester were 62 BUT 9612Ts with Burlingham bodywork delivered in 1955-56. Ironically, the first conversions to bus operation took place the same year and these vehicles were destined for a short operating life. No 1322 was photographed leaving Every Street for Great Ancoats Street. One of the batch, No 1344, is also preserved. *Author*

Mexborough & Swinton

Left: The first two sections of trolleybus route operated by Mexborough & Swinton opened in 1915. Built to supplement the company's existing tramway, it was only in the 1920s (when agreement was reached with Rotherham over through working) that the trolleybus system was secure. The company's trams were replaced and the original routes upgraded. The final extension was completed in 1934. Although new vehicles were acquired until 1950, the system did not expand and, following the first conversion to bus operation in 1954, a gradual but inexorable decline ensued. The final services were operated on 27 March 1961, bringing to an end the history of company-owned trolleybuses in Britain.

The Mexborough & Swinton fleet was, throughout its 46-year history, exclusively comprised of single-deck vehicles. Typical of the fleet in its later years is Brush-bodied Sunbeam F4 No 27 of 1947 which was caught approaching Denaby Crossing just prior to the system's closure. *Michael Allen*

Above: The last vehicles to be acquired by the company were a trio of Brush-bodied Sunbeam F4s in 1950 — Nos 37-39. The first of the three is seen outside the small depot at Mexborough in the company of Nos 26 and 32. No 37 was one of 12 vehicles sold to Bradford upon withdrawal; seven, including No 37, were to be rebodied by East Lancs and were destined to become the last trolleybuses to enter service in Bradford. As Bradford No 845 this vehicle survives in preservation. Sister vehicle No 844 was to become Britain's official last trolleybus. *Michael Allen*

Newcastle-upon-Tyne

Left: Although investigations into the possible operation of trolleybuses occurred as early as 1911, it was not until 1935 that they first appeared. Adopted for tramway replacement, the system grew rapidly in the late 1930s and into the early years of World War 2. After the war extensions continued to be built until 1956, although the system was never as extensive as envisaged. Conversion of the network to bus operation commenced in June 1963 and was completed in October 1966. Initially, the system's livery was yellow, brown and cream, but this was later simplified to the familiar yellow and cream livery.

The entire fleet was replaced by Sunbeam F4s and BUTs (both 9641Ts and 9611Ts) between 1948 and 1950. No 488 was a Metro-Cammell-bodied BUT 9641T, one of a batch of 20 delivered between 1948 and 1949. For speed of delivery after World War 2 these vehicles were identical to the contemporary London 'Q1' class then being constructed at the same works. Similar vehicles were also supplied to Glasgow. *F. W. Ivey*

Below left: A second BUT 9641T with Metro-Cammell bodywork heads towards Central station on route No 31A. This route was a branch off the main route north to Gosforth Park and served the Grange Estate. Opened on 28 October 1951, this route was the penultimate extension in Newcastle and was to survive until February 1964. *Geoff Lumb*

Right: In 1950 Newcastle placed a batch of 50 BUT 9641Ts with Metro-Cammell bodywork in service. These vehicles, No 579-628, were destined to become the last trolleybuses to enter service in the city. No 590 is pictured on route No 43. Sister vehicle No 628, the last trolleybus delivered to the city, is one of two Newcastle trolleybuses to survive in preservation. *Photobus/A. Douglas*

Nottingham

Above: The City of Nottingham possessed one of the largest trolleybus systems in the country. Although first thoughts of trolleybus operation dated back to before World War 1, it was only in the mid-1920s, when facing tramway replacement, that the trolleybus made its début. The first route opened in 1927 and expansion was rapid thereafter. However, the last tramway conversions, in 1936, were to motorbus and no trolleybus extensions were constructed after 1935. The Notts & Derby system, which ran over the Corporation's overhead into central Nottingham, was converted to bus operation in 1953, but the abandonment of the Corporation network did not commence until 1962. The last route was converted to bus operation in June 1966.

By 1952 the entire prewar fleet had been replaced by more than 150 trolleybuses delivered between 1943 and 1952. These vehicles were supplied by Sunbeam, Karrier and BUT, whilst bodywork was produced by Weymann, Park Royal, Roe and Brush. No 454 was one of three Karrier Ws with Park Royal Utility bodywork supplied in 1944. *F. W. Ivey*

Right: Caught operating on route No 40 to Wilford Bridge on 28 March 1964, No 478 was one of a batch of 10 Park Royal-bodied Karrier Ws delivered to Nottingham in 1946. *Geoff Lumb*

Left: No 521 was one of 25 8ft-wide Brush-bodied BUT 9611Ts delivered in 1949 and 1950. It is pictured turning from King Street into Queen Street on the Mansfield Road route — the last service to operate — weeks before the final closure. Sister vehicles Nos 502 and 506 are preserved. *Author*

Above: The last trolleybuses delivered to Nottingham were a batch of 77 BUT 9641Ts with Brush bodywork delivered in 1951-52. One of these 70-seat vehicles, No 549, is seen operating on route No 43 to Trent Bridge via Arkwright Street. This route was converted to bus operation on 1 April 1965. Sister vehicle No 578 is preserved. *Photobus/A. Richardson*

Portsmouth

Left: Although trolleybuses had been considered as tram replacements for several years, it was not until 1934 that the first route commenced operation. Over the next two years the entire tramway network disappeared and by 1938 the fleet stood at 100 trolleybuses. The immediate postwar years saw both extensions and a number of withdrawals, although only 15 new vehicles were acquired after the war. Although definite conversion proposals were adopted in 1956, actual abandonment did not start to take place until 1960. The system was converted to bus operation in five stages, with the last vehicles operating on 27 July 1963.

The largest batch of trolleybuses acquired by Portsmouth were 76 AEC 661Ts with Craven bodywork delivered in 1936-37. One of this batch, No 297 (originally numbered 97), is seen on route No 18 towards Eastney.
Julian Thompson

Reading

Right: The Berkshire town of Reading was for many years regarded as one of the country's most secure trolleybus operators; indeed, the final batch of vehicles was not placed in service until 1961 and the last extension completed in 1963, but the policy changed and the system was converted to bus operation between 1965 and November 1968. The system's origins dated back to the 1930s, when the Corporation was seeking replacements for its tramway fleet. The first route opened in 1936 and the final trams disappeared in May 1939.

The final demise of the trams was facilitated by the acquisition of a batch of 25 AEC 661Ts, Nos 107-31, which entered service during 1939. This was the operator's first significant delivery of trolleybuses, and followed on from six test vehicles acquired to inaugurate the first route in 1936. No 112 is seen in Mill Lane depot — a building which was constructed to house the tramway replacement fleet. Sister vehicle, No 113, was to become one of the first trolleybuses acquired for preservation by the Reading Transport Society (later British Trolley-bus Society) when it was withdrawn.
Geoff Lumb

Above: In 1961 Reading Corporation acquired a batch of 12 Sunbeam F4As with Burlingham bodywork. These were, however, destined to be the last vehicles acquired by the operator and were only to survive seven years in their home town. No 186, seen *en route* to Tilehurst, shows the attractive lines of the modern Burlingham body to good effect. On withdrawal, five of the type, Nos 183-86 and 192, were sold to Teesside, where they survived for a further three years. No 186, as Teesside T291, survives in preservation, as does sister vehicle No 193 in its original Reading condition. *Geoff Lumb*

Rotherham

Below: The South Yorkshire town of Rotherham could lay claim to possessing the fourth trolleybus system to operate in Britain, with services commencing on the Maltby route in 1912. Major expansion, however, only came in the 1930s when the bulk of the town's tramway system was converted to either bus or trolleybus operation. The one tram route to survive until after 1945 — the link to Templeborough — was the home to the trolleybus-like single-ended tramcars. One of the most unusual aspects of the Rotherham system was that, until a programme of rebodying in 1956-57, all the trolleybuses operated were single-deck. Although the first route to be converted to bus operation succumbed in 1954, it was not until 1962 that conversion became official policy. The last services were withdrawn in October 1965.

Typical of Rotherham's fleet of single-deck trolleybuses is this Daimler CTC6 with East Lancs bodywork, one of a total of 44 supplied between 1949 and 1951. Originally fleet number 77, this trolleybus had been renumbered 8 in 1956. Twenty of the type, but not No 77, were rebodied as double-deckers in 1956-57. *Michael Allen*

Left: No 40 started life in 1950 as a single-deck Daimler identical to No 8 seen in the previous illustration. Indeed, until renumbered when rebodied, No 40 was originally numbered 8! The decision to rebody the single-deckers was an effort to improve the finances of the system. The work was carried out by Roe. It was reasonably successful and ensured that the Rotherham network saw its 50th anniversary. A number of the redundant single-deckers were to be sold for further operation to Spain. Two of the rebodied double-deckers, No 37 and 44, survive in preservation; indeed, No 44 was to take part in the closure of the Manchester system in 1966. *F. W. Ivey*

St Helens

Above: From 1927 onwards the Lancashire town of St Helens was to see its small tramway network replaced by, primarily, trolleybuses. In 1931 the Corporation's wires met those of the adjacent South Lancashire Transport and this allowed for the joint operation of a route between the town and Atherton. The final trams operated in 1936 and St Helens now possessed a fleet of some 40 vehicles. Although further routes were proposed, only one extension (completed in 1943) was built. In 1950-51 a total of 16 new trolleybuses entered service; however, the following year the decision was made to convert the network to bus operation and closure was finally achieved in June 1958.

Pictured on 14 June 1958, a fortnight before final closure, No 381 awaits departure with a service for Rainhill. This was the last of eight Sunbeam F4s delivered in 1950-51. After closure the entire batch was sold to South Shields. The eight contemporary BUT 9611Ts were sold to Bradford and one of the latter survives as the only ex-St Helens trolleybus in preservation. *John Senior*

South Lancashire Transport

Above: The South Lancashire Tramways Co constructed a large tramway network in the area to the west of Manchester, serving towns such as Bolton and Leigh and linking up with St Helens in the west. Powers were obtained in 1929 to convert the system to trolleybus operation and the first trolleybuses were introduced the following year. Although owning a significant route mileage — a total of some 30 miles in all — SLT only ever possessed 71 trolleybuses, of which four were actually owned by Bolton Corporation. The conversion of the system, a subsidiary of Lancashire United Transport, was announced in 1955 and the final trolleybus ran on 1 September 1958.

The first trolleybuses supplied to SLT were 10 Guy BTXs with Roe bodywork that were in stock for the opening of the Atherton-Ashton-in-Makerfield service in August 1930. The majority of this batch was rebuilt during the period 1950-56 and No 1, pictured as rebuilt, was photographed at Swinton depot on 10 August 1958. *John Senior*

Below: A further batch of three-axle Guy BTXs, Nos 11-30, followed before 16 two-axle Guy BTs, again with Roe bodywork, were obtained in 1933. No 34, seen *en route* for Atherton on 23 June 1957, was one of those that were not rebuilt in the early 1950s. The increasingly aged Guys looked out of date even in the 1950s; it is a crying shame that the trolleybus preservation movement started only after these remarkable examples had all been scrapped. *John Senior*

Left: The last vehicles that SLT acquired before the outbreak of World War 2, and the first that were not produced by Guy, were 12 Leyland TTB4s with Roe bodywork, Nos 48-59. These were delivered between 1935 and 1938 and were the only Leyland trolleybuses in the fleet as well as the last to be supplied to the operator with Roe bodywork. Subsequent deliveries were of Karriers and Sunbeams and all were fitted with Weymann bodies. No 53 was photographed at Spinning Jenny Street, in Leigh, on 16 August 1958. *John Senior*

South Shields

Above: Trolleybuses reached the northeast town of South Shields in 1935, when the form of transport was adopted for tramway replacement. A significant network was constructed before the outbreak of World War 2 and further extensions in the postwar years saw the system reach its peak in 1948. Although no new vehicles were acquired after 1950, second-hand examples were acquired from both Pontypridd and St Helens in the late 1950s. In 1958 the first withdrawal took place and full conversion

became policy the following year. The last trolleybus operated in April 1964.

Here No 262, a 1950 Karrier F4 with Northern Coach Builders bodywork, is seen with the North Sea and the South Pier, as a backdrop showing the aspect of the town as a popular coast resort. No 262 was one of a batch of 10 Karriers acquired in 1950 that were the last new trolleybuses delivered to the system. *F. W. Ivey*

Above: A long-forgotten sight is the wooden seating of Utility bodywork built during World War 2. Here we see the interior of No 236, a Park Royal-bodied Karrier W4 that came second-hand from Pontypridd in 1957. Materials were, of course, in short supply during the war, and bodybuilders often had to resort to unseasoned wood — the principal bodybuilding material of the day. Consequently, in later life, these bodies were often rebuilt or replaced and, in this case, evidence of rebuilding can be seen where the front windows and window frames have been replaced. Unusually, though, the wooden seats have survived, just waiting to snag belt-buckles from contemporary raincoats just as you were about to stand up in readiness to get off. Remember, though, that these seats were eminently serviceable. *F. W. Ivey*

Right: Another aspect of South Shields environment is industry, trade and shipping as seen here at Tyne Dock. No 203 was the second vehicle in the fleet to carry this number; the first No 203 was one of the original Karriers that inaugurated the system in 1935. This particular vehicle came from St Helens in 1958. Originally numbered 176 (and renumbered 376 in 1955), this was one of a batch of Sunbeam F4s with East Lancs bodywork delivered in 1950-51. *Michael Allen*

Teesside Railless Traction Board

Left: Close to the town of Middlesbrough are the small industrial towns of North Ormsby, South Bank, Normanby and Eston, settlements which were home to a small — but historically important — trolleybus network for more than 50 years, dating originally to September 1919. Although relatively small, the Teesside system can lay claim to being one of only two systems that did not have an origin in a local tramway operation (the other being Ramsbottom), whilst with the linking of the Normanby and Grangetown routes in 1968 the TRTB opened the last trolleybus extension in the country. However, 1968 was also to see the TRTB merged within Teesside Municipal Transport and the trolleybus system threatened. The final obsequies occurred on 4 April 1971.

Prior to the creation of TMT in 1968, the TRTB livery was dark green. It is seen here on No 6, one of seven Sunbeam F4s delivered in 1950, on 16 April 1960. As pictured here, the Sunbeam was fitted with an East Lancs body, but the entire batch was rebodied by Roe between 1962 and 1965. Sister vehicle No 5 is preserved. *Geoff Lumb*

Above: The final vehicles acquired by Teesside were five of the 1961 vintage Sunbeam F4As with Burlingham body, which had been rendered surplus to requirements in Reading. These entered service in 1969 under the auspices of TMT and appeared in the new owner's turquoise livery. No 9 is pictured outside South Bank depot on 27 April 1969. It was later to be renumbered T289. Also visible in the background is the photographer's well-known preserved Guy Wolf. One of the ex-Reading vehicles, No T291, survives in preservation. *Geoff Lumb*

Walsall

Left: The first route in this West Midlands town was a replacement service that led to the reintroduction of the through service to Wolverhampton that had been severed some years earlier when the latter town had adopted trolleybuses. Although Walsall's system was inaugurated in the summer of 1931, it was only in November that through services were restored. Although there were further developments to the system, it was only the appointment of a new General Manager, the redoubtable R. Edgley Cox, in 1952 that saw major expansion. The system doubled in size between 1955 and 1963 when several of the heavily-trafficked local routes were converted. Experimentation also took place with vehicles and some strange rebuilds resulted. In 1969 Walsall passed to the newly-created West Midlands Passenger Transport Executive and, despite opposition, the new operators quickly dispensed with the trolleybuses; the last ran on 3 October 1970.

Photographed turning outside St Paul's church, by the town centre bus station, is No 339, a Brush-bodied Sunbeam F4 that was delivered in 1950. *Author*

Above: The second-coming of Walsall's trolleybuses in the late 1950s and early 1960s saw many second-hand trolleybuses arrive in the town. These acquisitions included No 876, which had been originally Cleethorpes No 61 before arriving in Walsall in 1960. This BUT had Northern Coach Builders bodywork, of a design that looked remarkably similar to contemporary ECW bodies as a result of a key member of staff moving from Lowestoft to Newcastle. However, the fertile mind of R. Edgley Cox was never still, and a considerable number of trolleybuses in the fleet were altered to a greater or lesser extent; together with two others of the batch No 876 ended up nothing at all like its original designers had intended, being extended to 30ft in length and converted to a front-entrance. Symbolically it is seen at the Beechdale Estate terminus with the Walsall power station as a backdrop. *Author*

Left: No 850 is another ex-Cleethorpes vehicle, in this case a Roe-bodied Crossley 'Empire' dating from 1951. Numbered 63 in the Cleethorpes fleet, it was one of two delivered that year — the last new vehicles to be acquired by the east coast operator. Unlike many of the other trolleybuses in Walsall, No 850 survived until the 1970s in virtually an unaltered form. *Author*

Above: The purpose-built bus station at St Paul's Street was a rarity in the British trolleybus world. Parked here, apart from Crossley No 850, are two of the 22 Sunbeam F4As, with unusual Willowbrook bodywork, that were delivered between 1954 and 1956. These vehicles represented the backbone of the Walsall fleet until final closure, and were notable in being the first 30ft long vehicles on two axles; No 851 actually entered service, to much acclaim, prior to the necessary regulation being enacted. Three of these unusual vehicles survive into preservation. *Author*

Wolverhampton

Above: It must not be thought that the neighbouring town of Walsall was by any means unusual in having its operation headed by a well-known and respected General Manager; amongst several others that come to mind are F. Canuder in Cardiff and Charles Owen Silver at Wolverhampton. Of all the proponents of the trolleybus, the latter perhaps did more than any other individual to bring the 'trolleybus' out of the 'trackless' era to enable it to become an exceptionally fine form of transport.

Trolleybuses had first operated in Wolverhampton in 1923 and the system expanded rapidly through to the 1930s, by which stage it had virtually reached its peak. New vehicles continued to be acquired until 1949, although a number of older vehicles were rebodied during the 1950s. The first closure occurred in early 1961 and conversion soon became official policy; the last trolleybus ran on 5 March 1967.

One of the system's most important routes was the joint service linking it to neighbouring Walsall. Here examples of the two fleets are seen on an enthusiasts' tour. Wolverhampton No 649, a Guy BT with Park Royal bodywork, was one of the final batch of trolleybuses delivered. Sister vehicle No 654 is preserved. *F. W. Ivey*

Right: After the delivery of the last batch of all-new trolleybuses in 1949, a number of older vehicles were rebodied by Charles H. Roe in Leeds. Amongst those so treated was No 439, originally a Park Royal-bodied Sunbeam W of 1947. It is also seen on an enthusiasts' tour, this time at Tettenhall. *F. W. Ivey*